Who
Will I Serve?

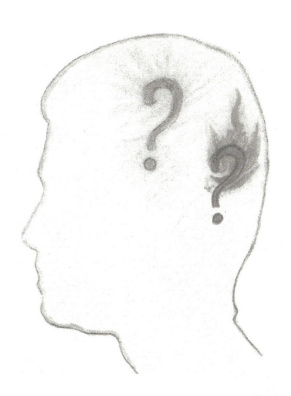

Enrique T. Martinovic

ISBN 978-1-0980-7988-8 (paperback)
ISBN 978-1-0980-7989-5 (digital)

Christian Faith Publishing, Inc.
832 Park Avenue
Meadville, PA 16335
www.christianfaithpublishing.com

Translated from the original Spanish title, *A Quién Serviré?*
Translator: Enrique T. Martinovic
Front Cover Design: Marta D. Martinovic
Other works available from the same author:
Adam, the Unknown
Original Spanish title:
Adán el Desconocido
Biblical Scripture taken from the New King James Version

Printed in the United States of America

Contents

Preface

The author of this book shares a personal experience that changed his life both emotionally and spiritually.

The Word of God says, "*My people are destroyed for lack of knowledge*" (Hosea 4:6).

Therefore, when we discover in the verses of the word of God, all that He wants to teach us. Then true freedom begins. "*But now having been set free from sin, and having become slaves of God, you have your fruit to holiness, and the end, everlasting life*" (Romans 6:22).

Chapter 1

Why Serve?

Who wants to think about serving? We live surrounded by examples of people that serve in our society in different ways.

Have you ever needed to take a trip to the local supermarket to buy milk? Consider the people involved to make it possible for you to buy that milk. Consider those employees at that store, available to serve you.

When you stop at a restaurant to order your favorite meal, keep in mind all those employees who work only to serve you your dinner, starting with the host who greets you at the door, to the waiter who takes your order, the cooks who prepare your food, and an entire staff of people all there to serve you.

The fact is that every day, we live surrounded with examples of people that continuously serve. And let's not forget the police, the firefighters, or the military. They are constantly attending to our security with their protection and dedication to our well-being. They are serving. We refer to them as civil servants.

In my opinion, there has never been more slaves in this world than in these days. I am referring specifically to the slavery to credit cards.

I will not overwhelm you with statistics of how many credit cards there are today in the country. I know that you will agree with me that there is no greater slavery than the slavery to credit cards. The banks that issue these cards do so with a very low initial interest rate known as "a teaser" or introductory rate.

Later, they will charge you with different fees such as penalize interest. They did it with me in 1981.

Proverbs 22:7 says, *"The rich rules over the poor and the borrower is servant to the lender."*

Chapter 2

Journey to the Past

To understand the causes of slavery, we must travel to the past to the book of Genesis after creating the earth. In the Garden of Eden, key events unfolded. Events that determined the future of humanity. God created man in His image and likeness.

> *"Let Us make man in Our Image, according to Our likeness; let them have dominion over the fish of the sea, over the birds of the air, and over the cattle, over all of the earth and over every creeping thing that creeps on the earth"* (Genesis 1:26).

In the Bible, God reveals why and for what purpose He created man. God created man for His glory, His delight, and to serve Him.

First.

The crowning point of God's creation on earth. A living human being molded from earth's dust and being formed according to the image of God, his Creator. Also given His likeness by the spirit.

> *"And the Lord God formed man of the dust of the ground, and breathed into his nostrils the breath of life; and man became a living being"* (Genesis 2:7).

After creating man, God decides that Adam should not be alone.

And the Lord God said, *"It is not good that man should be alone. I will make him a helper comparable to him"* (Genesis 2:18).

Second.

God gave man authority over the planet and all His creation on it.

> *"Then God blessed them, and God said to them, 'Be fruitful and multiply; fill the earth and subdue it; have dominion over the fish of the sea, over the birds of the air, and over every living thing that moves on the earth '"* (Genesis 1:28).

Adam had authority and dominion over the planet. The words *subdue it* confirms the magnitude of Adam's authority on the planet. He could even command the weather. So the wind and rain with its clouds were at his command and pleasure.

God had made Adam god of planet earth with all the rights and attributes belonging to him.

Third.

God gave Adam authority over all the animal kingdom for man to rule over them. God brought to Adam the animals to name them according to their size, function, and species.

By naming them, Adam revealed his intelligence and sealed his authority and leadership over them.

> *"Out of the ground the Lord God formed every beast of the field, every bird of the air and brought them to Adam to see what he would call them. And whatever Adam called each living creature. That would be its name"* (Genesis 2:19).

I believe that includes extinct species such as dragons and dinosaurs.

Fourth.

The Bible teaches us that Adam was a friend of God.

> *And they heard the sound of the Lord God walking in the garden in the cool of the day... Then the Lord God called to Adam and said to him, "Where are you?"* (Genesis 3:8–9)

> *But you, Israel, are My servant, Jacob whom I have chosen, the descendants of Abraham My friend* (Isaiah 41:8)

It's very important to notice that God's purpose in creating man was to have friendship with Him. He already had thousands of angels to obey His commands, but He had not a friend.

Fifth.

God created man to serve Him.

> *"So you shall serve the Lord your God, and He will bless your bread and your water. And I will take sickness away from the midst of you"* (Exodus 23:25).

Just by holding God to His promise, we are assured a prosperous and healthy life all of our lives.

> *"And Jesus answered and said to him, 'Get behind Me, Satan! For it is written, You shall worship the Lord your God, and Him only you shall serve'"* (Luke 4:8).

Jesus defeated Satan's temptation by quoting the word of God. If we also quote God's word, we will defeat Satan's temptations.

Chapter 3

The Fall

Adam and Eve had authority to govern earth and exercise dominion over the planet and all that lived in it. It was God's commandment.

Satan wanted to make Adam fall since man and his wife were both one. If they did, they will lose the authority that they had on earth. Consequences of their fall would reach us their descendants. Satan was cast out of heaven by God because of his rebellion.

> *How you are fallen from heaven, O Lucifer, son of the morning! How you are cut down to the ground. You who weakened the nations! For you have said in your heart: I will ascend into heaven, I will exalt my throne above the stars of God; I will also sit on the mount of the congregation. On the farthest sides of the north; I will ascend above the heights of the clouds, I will be like the Most High.'*

Yet you shall be brought down to Sheol.
To the lowest depths of the Pit. (Isaiah
14:12–15)

Satan now sees Adam and his wife on earth in Eden where he used to be. Satan knew that he could not approach Adam and tempt him. If he could, he would have done it long ago. Now the woman was with Adam. Everything changed. Now there was someone who had the physical, emotional, and spiritual bond with Adam.

> *"Then the serpent said to the woman*
> *you will not surely die. For God knows*
> *that in the day you eat of it, your eyes*
> *will be opened, and you will be like God,*
> *knowing good and evil"* (Genesis 3:4–5).

All that was needed was the perfect time and place. Eve had to be alone without her husband support to help her reject the temptation.

> *"For Adam was formed first, then*
> *Eve. And Adam was not deceived, but the*
> *woman being deceived fell into trans-*
> *gression"* (1 Timothy 2:13–14).

The fall was accomplished in both sides. Eve was supposed to talk with Adam about the serpent's offer. Instead she decided it was good looking to her eyes and desirable.

In Genesis 3:6, the next thing she did was to eat the fruit. She took the initiative in acting upon herself without consulting her husband. She assumed a position of leadership that didn't belong to her. It should have been Adam's decision to make. Adam, by obeying his wife's voice and eating the fruit, failed to uphold his leadership and plunged all humanity into sin and death.

Then to Adam, He said, *"Because you have heeded the voice of your wife, and have eaten from the tree of which I commanded you, saying, 'You shall not eat of it'"* (Genesis3:17).

Eve spoke to Adam and convinced him to eat the fruit of the tree.

The subtle words used by Satan to deceive the woman, to make her believe that they could be equal to God. They were already like God on earth.

They were created by God. Not only did they have the physical image that God gave them, they also had His likeness. That implies to be eternal as God is. Nevertheless, they were totally innocent as children since they knew no evil until eating the fruit. Everything they could ever want or desire, they already had it.

By eating the fruit of the tree, Adam and his wife acted in disobedience to God, bringing death to their lives and ours. What they didn't know was that they represented the whole human race.

In that precise moment, after they ate the fruit, the clock of time started running forward in their lives. They began to age. God's sentence to Adam, *"But of the tree of the knowledge of good and evil you shall not eat, for in the day that you eat of it you shall surely die*" (Genesis 2:17).

It came to pass exactly as God had warned him. Adam died of 930 years of age. Seventy years short of one thousand. That is before a thousand years.

In God's calendar, a THOUSAND years is as ONE day.

> *"But, beloved, do not forget this one thing, that with the Lord one day is as a thousand years, and a thousand years as one day"* (2 Peter 3:8).

Everything that God had granted them, they lost it. Now Adam had to live the consequence of his disobedience.

> *Then the devil, taking him up on a high mountain, showed Him all the kingdoms of the world in a moment of time. And the devil said to Him, "All this authority will I give you, and their glory; for this has been delivered to me, and I give it to whomever I wish. Therefore, if you will worship before me, all will be yours." And Jesus answered and said to him, "Get behind Me, Satan! For it is written, you shall worship the Lord your God, and Him only you shall SERVE.* (Luke 4:5–8)

When Satan tells Jesus of the authority that he had over all the kingdoms of the world, what was he referring to?

It was a direct reference to what Adam had transferred to Satan. The jurisdiction to govern earth and all its creation in it. Adam had it, but by disregarding God's commandment, Adam brought sin and death to us all.

> *Therefore, just as through one man sin entered the world, and death through sin, and thus death spread to all men, because all sinned.* (Romans 5:12)

> *For since by man came death, by Man also came the resurrection of the death. For as in Adam all die, even so in Christ all shall be made alive.* (1 Corinthians 15:21–22)

Chapter 4

My Life

My life is not extraordinary. Nevertheless, it is important to me since it is my life. I lived the very first years of my life with my parents in the city of Santa Fe. It is the capital of the province of the same name in Argentina. While we were living in Santa Fe, before I reached the age of five, my parents drove me to a Catholic monastery in a town called Chovet.

Catholicism was my father's religion. They referred to it as a monastery, but I always called it a convent. My father was born in Croatia, one of the six republics of Yugoslavia. He spent the first fourteen years of his life in a convent himself. His mother passed away, and my grandfather was left with three boys (my father was the oldest), whom he could not apparently raise by himself.

My grandfather was a very wealthy man. In his early years, Tomas, my grandfather, started working for some nobleman. He was a member of the aristocracy. According to my father, he owned several businesses and would have been considered a millionaire. At the time of his death, my grandfather owned thirty-nine properties throughout Europe. One of them was a castle. That was my father's recollection that he shared with me when he came to visit me and my family in Long Beach, California, in 1993.

According to my father, my grandfather decided that his career in business was more important than his role as a father to his sons. That is why my father was placed in a convent to be raised and educated by priests. When the time came for my education, since my father was raised in a convent, he decided that it also was the best place to educate me. So at the age of five, I was placed in a convent.

I remember that we were 150 boys living in that convent. Of all the children there, I was the only boy whose father and mother were still alive. All the other children were orphans of their fathers, and many had also lost their mothers in the second world war, fighting against the German invasion to their homeland. I lived a year in that convent. It was a very painful year. Being a five-year-old boy taken out of his house for no reason at least to my mind, separated of his only known family at such a young age.

I felt desperation out of my regular family environment. We were four in my family. My father, Santiago (his real name was Jacob Kristo), my mother, Carmen, my sister, Cristina, and myself. We were not a big family, but that was my family, and there was no way that I could conceive the idea of life without them.

The only thought that I remember to justify my staying in the convent was to learn my father's language, the Croat dialect. They taught me to speak, read, and write Croat. I remember how I used to cry for days on end as I missed my family, especially my mother with whom I had a special attachment, because I was suffering of loneliness.

I decided that when I grow up and get married, I will not have children that will grow without brothers and sisters in their lives as I did.

At the convent, they gave me a mouse-gray uniform. That is how I called it, and still do.

In the convent, that was the color of the uniforms we wore. Two or three times a week, we had to walk to the church for mass in the freezing night.

We were altar boys. We had to walk to the other end of town very early in the morning to help the priest at the 6:00 a.m. Mass. I remember one very special Sunday. My parents came to visit me. I was so happy. Imagine my parents came to visit me. To the other children, it was a sad event. They had no fathers, and many of them had no parents at all. All they had was grandparents, and it was very sad for them. Nevertheless, it was a very happy occasion for me, and I decided that I was going to enjoy their visit enormously. The problem came in the afternoon at about four or five. My parents were leaving, and I was left behind.

They said goodbye and took the train back home. I thought that they were going to take me with them to return home, but I was wrong. They returned home without me. They left me at the convent. My only consolation was to cry myself to sleep. I felt then as sad as the other children.

What scared me the most about that convent was the teacher we had. As I remember, he was the teacher that we had for the Croat language, but he also taught all the other subjects (arithmetic, history, and so on). The reason that this teacher was terrifying was his gaze. He would look, and it would appear as if he wanted to pierce you with his eyes. At least that was the impression that remained in my memory. Through the eyes of a five-year-old, he was a fearful giant and our worst nightmare. Whenever I didn't pay attention in the class or made mistakes in my assignments, punishment would follow. If there was a thing that none of us wanted, it was to be punished.

I remember two different types of punishment that this teacher would give us every time that we made a mistake, and at five years of age, you make mistakes every day.

One of the punishments would be to gather all the fingers of one hand pointing up as if making a pyramid. Then with his pointer, he would hit us right in the top were all the fingers gathered together. It caused a sharp pain that caused a crippling numbness to surge through your entire hand that sometimes lasted all day.

The second punishment would be to make us kneel in a corner in front of the classroom. The corner would be sprayed with dried corn grains.

As you can imagine, the pain was unbearable. Every one of us would cry in pain. This would only make him angrier than before the punishment began. Finally, the year passed. I returned to my house and to my family. One of the priests named Paulino took me home in a bus. I thought that we were going back to Santa Fe, the city where we used to live when I went to the convent. Instead, we went to Rosario. That was where my parents had moved with my sister, Cristina. Rosario was bigger than Santa Fe. Besides it was closer to Buenos Aires, the capital and more advantageous for my father's business. Once I settled in my home, I started elementary school. Back in those years, we started school at the age of six, which was for the first year, or as we called it, first grade, then year after year until we reached the sixth grade (last year of our elementary studies). By the time I finished my third grade year, I had many friends and lots of fun but very low school grades. Then again, my father decided that I needed to change schools to reach better grades and have a better education. I was transferred to another public school where I spent my fourth-grade year. It was a disaster for me. I didn't like it.

I felt like a foreigner there, and I fell sick constantly. Of course, by then, I had lost all the friends I had. I felt very lonely. I could not make friends in the neighborhood. The area where we lived was mostly commercial.

My next school was the Salesian School of Don Bosco. It was a Catholic school. There I ended my last two years of elementary studies.

During that process, I was being educated into the Catholic religion. In my personal opinion, it is one of the most comfortable religions that I had ever known of at that time. If you committed a sin (and who doesn't), then all you have to do is to go to the priest and tell him your sin. It's called confession. He will give you the penance (usually four or five prayers, depending in the seriousness of the sin). That is all you have to do.

You are done. Forgiven by God (that is according to them). And this is because, according to the Catholic religion, the priests have the right to forgive you your sins (at least that's how it was when I was a young catholic). It was as if that priest was the one who died at the cross of Calvary for our sins. Only Christ Jesus, the Son of God, has the power and the authority to forgive our sins.

Because against Him and Him only, we have sinned.

> *But He was wounded for our transgressions, He was bruised for our iniquities. The chastisement of our peace was upon Him and by His stripes we are healed"* (Isaiah 53:5)

> *I acknowledge my sin to You and my iniquity I have not hidden. I said, "I will confess my transgressions to the Lord."* *And You forgave the iniquity of my sin.* (Psalm 32:5)

Jesus died not only to give us eternal salvation but also to obtain healing to our bodies by His stripes in the post before His crucifixion at the cross.

> *But if the Spirit of Him who raised Jesus from the dead dwells in you, He who raised Christ from the dead will also give life to your mortal bodies through His Spirit who dwells in you.* (Romans 8:11)

We find how God forgives our sins upon confession to Him.

> *For the Father judges no one, but has committed all judgment to the Son, that all should honor the Son just as they honor the Father. He who does not honor the Son does not honor the Father who sent Him.* (John 5:22–23)

In these verses, we find who holds all judgment. It is the Lord Jesus Christ Himself.

> *The next day John saw Jesus coming toward him, and said, "Behold! The Lamb of God who takes away the sin of the world!"* (John 1:29)

Now then, we are ambassadors for Christ as though God were pleading through us we implore you on Christ behalf, be reconciled to God. For He made Him who knew no sin to be sin for us, that we might become the righteousness of God in Him. (2 Corinthians 5:20–21)

Chapter 5

A Nocturnal Revelation

In 1985, my wife, Marta, and I were living in California together with our seven children. By then, we had been married for twenty-two years. God had blessed us by bringing us to the United States. He gave us a beautiful family with three girls and four boys.

It was around that time that I had already read the Bible about two or three times from cover to cover.

My life was entirely consumed with providing for the needs that a family of nine people would have. I was working for the US postal service. I would work all the overtime hours I could get. One night, in 1985, I had a terrible dream. I dreamt that I was completely alone in a very dark street. I was standing in the middle of the street in this gloomy night. I felt very cold and very frightened. I saw coming toward me, two angels of darkness. They looked as if they were transparent, but their silhouette was black. They were coming directly toward me. I wanted to run, to flee out of there as fast as I could, but it was impossible for me to move. I wanted to start moving my legs toward the opposite direction from where they were coming, but it was useless. I was paralyzed. I wanted to scream, to shout as loud as possible, "HELP! Please! HELP ME!" but I could not release a single sound out of my mouth. My tongue was dried.

I could not even move my lips. I was totally paralyzed and helpless. I had no strength in my body to move, not even the slightest movement to attempt to flee out of such terrible situation. When they were near me, they positioned themselves one on each side of me. They lifted me up in the air by my armpits. They began to carry me away with my feet up in the air. I knew that they were carrying me to hell. My desperation was total.

I was completely paralyzed because of the proximity of these angels, depriving me of every chance to free myself. Inside of me, I felt this tremendous void, as if something had departed from within me. I felt this terrible feeling of emptiness inside me. I felt as if I was drowning.

I had within me the conviction of my condemnation. I knew that there was absolutely nothing that I could do. It was too late for me to do anything. It was too late for repentance. I knew that I had exceeded the period of grace, and there was no more time left to appeal. It was too late.

My destiny was with the eternal darkness, and I saw myself being carried to hell, to my condemnation. When I woke up, I could not believe that it was a dream. It had been so real to me. I understood the meaning of such a horrible revelation.

What God had given me to dream was my actual spiritual condition. I was lost. My true spiritual condition was not the one that I thought that I had been living.

I always thought, "Once saved, always saved." I never thought that after accepting the salvation that God gives us through His Son, Jesus, I could lose it. The truth is that salvation can be lost. I had forgotten the meaning that the warning of the Scriptures has in our spiritual lives. Paul the Apostle mentioned about the possibility of his own condemnation.

> *But I discipline my body and bring it into subjection. Lest, when I have preached to others, I myself should become disqualified.* (1 Corinthians 9:27)

Again he mentioned the dangers we have of losing our salvation.

> *Therefore, my beloved, as you have always obeyed. Not as in my presence only, but now much more in my absence, work out your own salvation with fear and trembling.* (Philippians 2:12)

The Lord Jesus says, "*He who overcomes, shall be clothed in white garments, and I will not blot out his name from the Book of Life; but I will confess his name before my Father and before His angels*" (Revelation 3:5).

We know that you cannot erase anything that had not been previously written. Therefore, my conclusion is that when I accepted Jesus Christ as my Lord and Savior, then I became saved and my sins were forgiven.

I was born again, and my name was written in the Book of Life. For my name to remain in the Book of Life, I need to overcome. In other words, I needed to win the daily battle that I must fight against the desires of my flesh and desires in my mind in order to retain the salvation that Jesus won for me at the cross.

> *Therefore, put to death your members which are on the earth: fornication, uncleanness, passion, evil desire, and covetousness, which is idolatry.* (Colossians 3:5)

> *Likewise you also, reckon yourselves to be dead indeed to sin, but alive to God in Christ Jesus our Lord.* (Romans 6:11)

I lived all those years with the inner confidence that I could not lose my salvation. But now, God showed me that I was lost into eternity, away from God and without Him.

Until that time, I thought that I had been this great Christian man, just because I was working so much and so hard to provide for my family everything that they needed. I had been a faithful husband to my wife.

I thought that all those that knew me thought that I was such a good, hardworking father and husband. I thought God would think the same of me. However, the life that I was living had not been the life that God wanted me to live. It was the life my mind wanted me to live. Spiritually we have a battleground in our body located in our head between our ears.

> *And you He made alive, who were dead in trespasses and sins, in which you once walked according to the course of this world, according to the prince of the power of the air, the spirit who now works in the sons of disobedience, among whom also we all once conducted ourselves in the lust of our flesh, fulfilling the desires of the flesh and of the mind and were by nature children of wrath, just as the others.* (Ephesians 2:1–3)

My life, in reality, was torture since I was blaming God for my depression and my frustrations.

Constantly, my wife and children shared with me my miserable life. They suffered because they did not know how to help me change my situation. But in the process, they felt guilty as if they were the cause of my pain. My anger was so widespread that I constantly was in my mind, holding everyone in judgment, including my coworkers. The reason varied from their size, color, rank, work ethic, or even behavioral patterns. Regardless of the cause, I was constantly judging them, whether they were relatives, acquaintances, close family, or anybody whose path crossed in my life.

Chapter 6

The Beginning of a New Life

Part 1

That struggle that I had inside me, the constant impulse to accuse by judging anybody, anytime, and anywhere starting with God. It had become a mental torture. Like a hammer, it pounded inside of my mind. I constantly had reasons to accuse anyone and anything that I judged was wrong. Always there was someone to blame but me.

> *Do not speak evil of one another, brethren. He who speaks evil of a brother and judges his brother, speaks evil of the law and judges the law. But if you judge the law, you are not a doer of the law but a judge. There is one Lawgiver, who is able to save and destroy. Who are you to judge another?* (James 4:11–12)

I was living a double life. Outwardly, mine was the life of a loving husband to his wife and family, totally dedicated to their well-being. Nothing was out of the normal life that any other man would live. But inward, it was completely different. There was another man living inside me. He commanded my life, not as I wanted it but as he wanted. That man was myself. It was my inner man. In the Bible, it is called the old man.

> *But you have not so learned Christ, if indeed you have heard Him and have been taught by Him, as the truth is in Jesus; that you put off, concerning your former conduct, the old man which grows corrupt according to the deceitful lusts, and be renewed in the spirit of your mind. And that you put on the new man which was created according to God, in true righteousness and holiness.*
> (Ephesians 4:20–24)

I was not suffering from dementia nor was I insane. There is a reality that we need to learn to identify. According to what God, in His word, teaches, I was a prisoner, and my MIND was my jail.

I needed to be liberated of that prison that was tormenting me. In other words, the enemy inserts in our mind a thought. We like it to the point where we consider it to be true. It's then when he builds a spiritual fortress in our thinking. It could be related to our health, our finances, our relationships, or our family. Satan always tries to enslave us.

> *For though we walk in the flesh, we do not war according to the flesh. For the weapons of our warfare are not carnal but mighty in God for pulling down strongholds, casting down arguments and every high thing that exalts itself against the knowledge of God, bringing every thought into captivity to the obedience of Christ.* (2 Corinthians 10:3–5)

That mental prison didn't allow me to have the life I wanted to have with my God, my wife, and my children.

> *Then Jesus said to those Jews who believed Him, "If you abide in my word, you are my disciples indeed. And you shall know the truth, and the truth shall make you free."* (John 8:31–32)

I was living in this spiritual fortress. My understanding had been blocked. I only knew that I wanted to escape of that constant "judgment mode" toward everyone that surrounded me. Nevertheless, having read the Word so many times, I did not live it. I needed the freedom that God offered me through Christ!

The freedom that His Word offered me had been blocked. I could not escape the spiritual blindness. We can read the Bible every day. But if we don't apply it in our daily life, with hunger to learn from the spirit of God, it will be as if we read the daily newspaper. The jail I was living was inside me, not in the physical sense but spiritual.

In the gospel of Matthew, the Lord Jesus tells a story of how we should forgive and also the consequences of not forgiving fullheartedly.

> *Then his master, after he had called him, said to him, you wicked servant! I forgave you all that debt because you begged me. Should you not also have had compassion on your fellow servant, just as I had pity on you? And his master was angry, and delivered him to the TORTURERS until he should pay all that was due to him.* (Matthew 18: 32–34)

I was confined into prison, not human but spiritual. I had pronounced a lot of judgment in my heart, against my wife, against my children, against my coworkers, and against my God. And because the excess of my sin, I had been blinded by the god of this world. That old serpent, which is the devil, and Satan.

> *But even if our gospel is veiled, it is veiled to those who are perishing, whose minds the god of this age has blinded, who do not believe, lest the light of the gospel of the glory of Christ, who is the*

image of God, should shine on them.
(2 Corinthians 4:3–4)

We could be converted Christians and yet unbelievers of the Word of God. Many times, I begged God to forgive my sins. But after two or three days, I was falling again in the same transgression. I knew that every time that I confessed my sin, God forgave me.

If we confess our sins, He is faithful and just to forgive us our sins, and to cleanse us from all unrighteousness. (1 John 1:9)

Most assuredly, I say to you, whoever commits sin is a slave of sin. (John 8:34)

I was a servant of sin. I was falling into the same pit, the same transgression, living within that vicious circle of sin. I would repent, and sin again.

Until one day, the Lord Jesus revealed to me a passage in the Bible that changed my life forever. It changed my relationship with HIM.

Let this mind be in you which was also in Christ Jesus, who, being in the form of God, did not consider it robbery to be equal with God, but made Himself of no reputation. Taking the form of

a bondservant, and coming in the like-
ness of men. And being found in appear-
ance as a man, He humbled Himself and
became obedient to the point of death,
even the death of the cross." (Philippians 2:5–8)

After reading this passage, I finally understood. To
live among men, Jesus Christ had to take the form of a
servant, a slave. Therefore, if Jesus made Himself a servant, a slave in order to become human, then all humans
are slaves.

All of us, men and women by having this human
body are servants, created by God to serve HIM. God
created me to serve Him. His will is that I serve Him.
Though it is God's will that I serve Him, He allows me
to decide to serve Him or not to serve Him.

One thing is certain. I will serve. To whom? That is
up to me, but be certain.

I will serve. Why? Because I am a human being, and
as a human, I was created to serve. Perhaps this is something too strong for someone to swallow, especially for
those living in their pride and arrogance. Always, in that
little corner of our mind, we have held that thought of "I
am the only master of my destiny." Or "I have the power
to rule my life."

Let us consider for a minute an automobile. It's a
vehicle created to ride on roads, paved or dirt, and for
long distances. However good, it is not suitable to travel
through rivers, oceans, or crossing continents. Another

example, we have the ship. This vessel was designed to travel across oceans. It cannot travel on a highway as a car would. As we understand the concept involving the design and creation of an automobile or a ship. It should be just as easy to understand the concept of the creation of man.

I, as a human being, was designed and created by God to serve Him and Him only. Jesus taught us who we should serve.

> *Then Jesus said to him, "Away with you, Satan! For it is written. You shall worship the Lord your God, and HIM only you shall serve."* (Matthew 4:10)

One may think, "I don't want to serve God, nor do I want to serve the devil." However, there is no neutral position. Jesus said, *"He who is not with me is against ME, and he who does not gather with ME, scatters abroad"* (Matthew 12:30).

If you don't want to serve God, you don't have to. God wants us to serve Him wholeheartedly and of our own free will. If not, then you are living to serve the flesh through your mind. That is what the devil wants, to control us through the mind.

> *No one can serve two masters; for either he will hate the one and love the other, or else he will be loyal to the one and despise the other.* (Mathew 6:24)

We read, *"Do you not know that to whom you present yourselves slaves to obey, you are that one's slaves whom you obey, whether of sin leading to death, or of obedience leading to righteousness?"* (Romans 6:16).

If, by deciding not to serve God, you think that you are also deciding not to serve the devil, you are mistaken. You will not serve him directly as a follower. That doesn't mean that you are not falling into his specific plans for you. Remember what happened with Adam and Eve?

Satan's plans for us are that we be very busy with the business of our daily life. This may include our family, our future, our studies, or our professional career. In other words, everything that is part of the flesh and life in this world or any distraction has nothing to do with God. Much less, anything that relates us to Jesus Christ. Satan doesn't want you to think in Jesus Christ because Jesus Christ is your savior for all eternity. Jesus defeated Satan at the cross, giving His life at Calvary. Satan does not want you to think about your spiritual life. Much less, in your death or what awaits you after death.

> *And as it is appointed for men to die once, but after this the judgment.* (Hebrews 9:27)

> *Blessed and holy is he who has part in the first resurrection. Over such the SECOND DEATH has no power, but they shall be priests of God and of Christ.* (Revelation 20:6)

It is in these things that Satan does not want you to ever think of. The Word of God is clear in its definition.

> *And you, being dead in your trespasses and the uncircumcision of your flesh, He has made alive together with Him, having forgiven you all trespasses. Having wiped out the handwriting of ordinances that was against us, which was contrary to us. And He has taken it out of the way, having nailed it to the cross. Having disarmed principalities and powers, He made a public spectacle of them, triumphing over them in it* (Colossians 2:13–15).

Unless you are rooted in the word of God, in your relationship with Christ, feeding your spirit in God's word, the devil can use you as a glove that fits in his hand. It moves and acts at his will becoming thereby an instrument of his plans for your own destruction.

If Satan succeeds in you not thinking of God or Jesus Christ today, he will accomplish his goal.

I was very excited to discover that God had created me to serve Him. Now I knew the purpose of my life. My very existence in this world was not an accident but planed by God.

There was a reason for me to be born. God allowed my birth because he wanted me to live for Him serving Him doing His will in my life.

Chapter 7

The Beginning of a New Life

Part 2

My first action after the dream and revelation was to confess to God my sin. I spent many years living in that condition of wrath and anger.

I acknowledged His authority over me. I also gave thanks to Jesus for His love and His patience. I did not kneel to ask forgiveness. I laid myself flat on the floor of my room as a sign of humility. I asked God out loud forgiveness for all my sins. I didn't spare any details to Him in my confessions. I cried out to Him, seeking forgiveness in the name of Jesus. I confessed to Jesus everything I had in my heart.

To confess our sins means to say, "Lord Jesus, I confess my sins to you." You don't need to remember each one of your sins. He already knows. The important part in confessing is to experience deep repentance within yourself, deciding not to continue in the old lifestyle.

> *For there is not a just man on earth*
> *who does good and does not sin.* (Eccle-
> siastes 7:20)

I also declared to him my will to live the rest of my life to serve Him.

My second decision after my confession was to gather my family in our living room. There, I confessed to them and asked for forgiveness. I started with my wife, Marta, then the children, starting with the oldest to the youngest. It is not easy for a man to humble and ask forgiveness. Believe me, it is not.

The Lord Jesus says, *"And whoever exalts himself will be humbled, and he who humbles himself will be exalted"* (Matthew 23:12).

> *The sacrifices of God are a broken*
> *spirit, a broken and a contrite heart.*
> *These, O God, You will not despise.*
> (Psalm 51:17)

> *The Lord is near to those who have*
> *a broken heart, and saves such as have*
> *a contrite spirit.* (Psalm 34:18)

After I finished asking forgiveness to my wife and children, I went to my place of work and asked my coworkers for their forgiveness. I approached them all one at a time. I confessed to them my faults. All of them forgave me with the exception of one man.

He said to me, "I will not forgive you. You may do it again tomorrow."

I answered him, "If I will do it again tomorrow or not that, I don't know. What I do know is that today, I ask your forgiveness, and you have refused to forgive me. My conscience is clean before God."

Within the following week, that man was fired from his job.

Chapter 8

The Beginning of a New Life

Part 3

Now that I had made peace with God, with my family and my coworkers, I needed to continue living my daily life. After all, only God knows when it will end. I decided not to continue to live my life as before. I seek refuge entirely in the reading of the Bible, feeding my soul with the Word.

I started a new method of daily reading. After work, before going to bed, I read a portion. However, I found it extremely difficult to achieve. My physical exhaustion was impossible to ignore. I could not concentrate in my reading.

My working schedule was three hours of overtime every day on top of my regular eight hours. By the time I arrived home, my body started to unwind. I had a limit of five to ten minutes of reading before falling asleep.

I needed to change my reading schedule to a different time and place. I decided to take my Bible to work and kept it in my locker. When my ten minutes of break time came, I would go to my locker and start my reading.

Since then, my life started to change. It was a new experience. It was as if I was diving into a pool that was the Word of God. That was how I took my daily readings. It was a complete and total surrender to the Lord and His word. While I was reading daily, I was also learning verses that I wanted to use to talk to God in my own and personal way. That led me to the creation of my prayer of deliverance. There is a difference between my Bible reading before my dream and now. It is to live what I read in the Bible. It says, *"For the Word of God is living and powerful, and Sharper than any two edged sword, piercing even to the division of soul and spirit, and of joints and marrow, and is a discerner of the thoughts and intents of the heart"* (Hebrews 4:12).

I discovered that what I should have done from the beginning was to scrutinize the word and examine how it applies in my personal life.

"And Jesus said to them, *'I am the bread of life. He who comes to me shall never hunger, and he who believes in me shall never thirst'* (John 6:35).

Finally, I started to comprehend that the Word of God is a daily food, Spiritual instead of physical. As such, indispensable for our survival. It is only in this manner that our spiritual man can prevail over our old carnal man.

I have a new bible reading system. I start by reading one of the gospels (my favorite is John). I start with Matthew until I finish. Then I follow with the book of

Acts. Later, the book of Romans. I continue with the next book until the end of the Bible in Revelations.

Since my reading was during my work breaks, by the time I finished the New Testament, six to eight months had passed. Through the daily reading and meditation of the word of God, our mind keeps a brisk memory of those verses that support us. This strengthens us in our faith.

Chapter 9

My Relationship with God

Daily prayer has become the most important and vital part of my relationship with God. I learned that the reading of the word of God is God's way of communicating with man. Through prayer, man communicates with God.

How frequently should we pray? Every day if possible, and many times, we want to speak to God.

> *Pray without ceasing.* (1 Thessalonians 5:16)

> *For there is not a word on my tongue, but behold, O Lord, You know it altogether.* (Psalm 139:4)

Search in the depth of your heart. Read the Bible. There are wonderful stories of people like us. They lived through challenges like we do today.

My advice is that you read the life of Jesus. I recommend you to start with the gospel of Luke. It is also important in our daily life to read the Epistles. They are letters which were written to Christian believers, to teach them how to live their daily lives in society. Those letters have teachings by the Holy Spirit for us to learn. In certain bibles, you find methods to read the entire Bible in a year.

When I am reciting my prayer, at the same time, I give to myself blessing, pouring into my life the promises contained in the verses I claim. While reading the Psalms, I have found wonderful promises of life, protection and health. I make those verses mine. I take them for me. I nibble them and eat them. I digest them, just as if they were food. I make them one in me as food. Part of my body, my soul, and my whole being. That is how I believe the Lord Jesus wants us to be with Him. *"One with Him; One in Him."*

In our younger years, we were dating our girlfriend. We always wanted to be with her, spend the most time sharing with her anything and everything because we loved her so much. We wanted to be near her all the time. So is with our Lord Jesus Christ.

> *Nevertheless I have this against you, that you have left your first love.* (Revelation 2:4)

Take the word as you would hold a sword to defend your life. To attack.

> *And take the helmet of salvation, and the sword of the Spirit, which is the word of God.* (Ephesians 6:17)

I defend every day my spiritual life. With the word of God, I attack those areas vulnerable in my life. I proclaim out of my mouth words of victory over them.

I stand at the door and knock. If anyone hears my voice and opens the door, I will come in to him and dine with him, and he with me. But him who is joined to the Lord is one spirit with Him. Now the Lord is the Spirit and where the Spirit of the Lord is, there is liberty. At that day you will know that I am in My Father, and you in me, and I in you. He who has my commandments and keeps them, it is he who loves me. And he who loves me will be loved by My Father, and I will love him and manifest myself to him. If anyone loves me, he will keep my word; and My Father will love him, and we will come to him and make our home with him. Now I am no longer in the world but these are in the world, and I come to You, Holy Father, keep through your name those you have given me, that they may be one as we are. That they all may be one, as You, Father, are in Me, and I in You; that they also may be one in Us, that the world may believe that You sent Me.

Now may the God of peace Himself sanctify you completely; and may your whole spirit, soul, and body be preserved blameless at the coming of our Lord Jesus Christ. I beseech you therefore, brethren, by the mercies of God, that you present your bodies a living sacrifice, holy acceptable to God which is your reasonable service. And do not be conformed to this world, but be transformed by the renewing of your mind, that you may prove what is that good and acceptable and perfect will of God. That the God of our Lord Jesus Christ, the Father of glory, may give to you the spirit of wisdom and revelation in the knowledge of Him, the eyes of your understanding being enlightened; that you may know what is the hope of His calling, what are the riches of the glory of His inheritance in the saints, and what is the exceeding greatness of His power toward us who believe, according to the working of His mighty power which He worked in Christ when He raised Him from the dead, and seated Him at His right hand in the heavenly places, far above all principality and power and might and dominion, and every name that it is named, not only in this age, but also in that which is to come. And He put all things under His feet, and gave Him to be head over all things to the church, which is His body, the fullness of Him who fills all in all. That He would grant you, according to

the riches of His glory, to be strengthened with might through His Spirit in
the inner man. Finally, my brethren, be
strong in the Lord and in the power of
His might. I want to pray everywhere,
lifting up holy hands, without wrath and
doubting. For God did not appoint us to
wrath, but to obtain salvation through
our Lord Jesus Christ. So let every man
be swift to hear, slow to speak, slow to
wrath; for the wrath of man does not
work the righteousness of God. Be anx-
ious for nothing, but in everything by
prayer and supplication, with thanksgiv-
ing, let your requests be made known to
God; casting all your care upon Him, for
He cares for you. And the peace of God,
which surpasses all understanding, will
guard your hearts and minds through
Christ Jesus. Finally, whatever things
are true, noble, just, and pure, if there
is any virtue, meditate on these things.
For though we walk in the flesh, we do
not war according to the flesh. For the
weapons of our warfare are not carnal
but mighty in God for pulling down
strongholds, casting down arguments
and every high thing that exalts itself
against the knowledge of God, bringing
every thought into captivity to the obedi-

ence of Christ. I affirm, by the boasting in you which I have in Christ Jesus our Lord, I die daily. I have been crucified with Christ; it is no longer I who live, but Christ lives in me; and the life which I now live in the flesh I live by faith in the Son of God, who loved me and gave Himself for me. And those who are Christ's have crucified the flesh with its passions and desires. Knowing this, that our old man was crucified with Him that the body of sin might be done away with that we should no longer be slaves of sin. For he who has died has been freed from sin. Now if we died with Christ, we believe that we shall also live with Him. Likewise, you also, reckon yourselves to be dead indeed to sin, but alive to God in Christ Jesus our Lord. For sin shall not have dominion over you, for you are not under law but under grace. And I say, for sin shall not have dominion over me, for I am not under the law but under grace. There is therefore now no condemnation to those who are in Christ Jesus, who do not walk according to the flesh, but according to the Spirit. For the law of the Spirit of life in Christ Jesus has made me free from the law of sin and death.

Therefore, if anyone is in Christ, he is a new creation; old things have passed away; behold, all things have become new. For we are His workmanship, created in Christ Jesus for good works, which God prepared beforehand that we should walk in them. He who believes in Me, as the Scripture has said, out of his heart will Flow Rivers of living waters. And I say, because I believe in You, Lord Jesus, out of my heart shall flow rivers of living waters. For the love of Christ compels us, because we judge thus; that if One died for all, then all died; and He died for all, that those who live should live no longer for themselves, but for Him who died for them and rose again. For none of us lives to himself, and no one dies to himself. For if we live, we live to the Lord, and if we die, we die to the Lord. Therefore, whether we live or die, we belong to the Lord.

Therefore, we do not lose heart. Even though our outward man is perishing, yet the inward man is being renewed day by day. But we are a chosen generation, a royal priesthood, a holy nation, His own special people, that we may proclaim the praises of Him who called us out of darkness into His marvelous light, having been born again, not of corruptible seed but incorruptible, through the word of God which lives and abides forever.

Rejoice always, pray without ceasing, and give thanks in everything for this is the will of God in Christ Jesus for you. And He open their understanding, that they may comprehend the Scriptures. And I say, and He opened my understanding that I may understand the Scriptures.

Moreover, by them your servant is warned, and in keeping them is great reward. Who can understand his errors? Cleanse me from secret faults.

Keep back your servant also from presumptuous sins; let them not have dominion over me. Then I shall be blameless, and I shall be innocent of great transgression. Let the words of my mouth and the meditation of my heart be acceptable in Your sight, O Lord, my strength and my Redeemer. Bless the Lord, O my soul, and all that is within me, bless His holy name! Bless the Lord, O my soul, and forget not all His benefits: who forgives all your iniquities, who heals all your diseases, who redeems your life from destruction, who crowns you with lovingkindness and tender mercy, who satisfies your mouth with good things. So that your youth is renewed like the eagle's. But thanks be to God, who gives us the victory through our Lord Jesus Christ.

The following verses are those I use in my daily prayer:

1 Corinthians 11:3
Matthew 6:24
Romans 6:16
James 4:7
Luke 9:23
John 12:26
Matthew 12:30
John 3:30
Galatians 5:22
Galatians 5:23
1 Peter 4:8
Luke 11:13
Luke11: 9–10
Revelation 3:20
1 Corinthians 6:17
2 Corinthians 3:17
John 14:20
John 14:21
John 14:23
John 17: 11

John 17: 21
1 Thessalonians 5:23
Romans 12:1–2
Ephesians 1:17–23
Ephesians 3:16
Ephesians 6:10
1 Timothy 2:8
1 Thessalonians 5:9
James 1:19–20
Philippians 4:6
1 Peter 5:7
Philippians 4:7–8
2 Corinthians 10:3–5
1 Corinthians 15:31
Galatians 2:20
Galatians 5:24
Romans 6:6
Romans 6:7
Romans 6:8
Romans 6:11
Romans 6:14
Romans 8:1–2
2 Corinthians 5:17
Ephesians 2:10
John 7:38
2 Corinthians 5:14
2 Corinthians 5:15
Romans 14:7
Romans 14:8
2 Corinthians 4:16

1 Peter 2:9
1 Peter 1:23
1 Thessalonians 5:16
1 Thessalonians 5:17
1 Thessalonians 5:18
Luke 24:45
Psalm 19:11
Psalm 19:12
Psalm 19:13
Psalm 19:14
Psalm 103:1
Psalm 103:2
Psalm 103:3
Psalm 103:4
Psalm 103:5
1 Corinthians 15:57

Chapter 11

Why I Use Those Verses and What They Mean to Me

1 Corinthians 11:3

I declare that Jesus Christ is my head and with it His Spiritual Jurisdiction over me.

Matthew 6:24

There is One God, But two spiritual Masters. We must decide who to serve.

Romans 6:16

It is a matter of choice in voluntary submission. A decision has to be made, wisely.

James 4:7

By submitting to Christ, we resist the devil because our focus is Christ. Satan is being ignored and must depart,

WHO WILL I SERVE?

flee from our side. It is a biblical promise that is fulfill.

Luke 9:23

We must become humble to follow Christ. Deny ourselves, pick up our cross (our destiny), and follow Him.

John 12:26

To serve Him, we must follow Him, every day. His promise is that we will be where He is, that is in His kingdom in Heaven.

Mathew 12:30

It's clear, if we are not with Christ, then we are against Him and His enemy.

John 3:30

Jesus must increase in my life so I could be His fully.

Galatians 5:22-3

I want the fruit of the Spirit to be in me every day, so I claim it.

1 Peter 4:8

If I am full of love to others, the promise is that it will cover an unspecified number of my sins.

Luke 11:13

The promise is for me to receive the Holy Spirit by asking in faith.

Luke 11:9-10

What I ask, seek, or call will be heard and answered.

Luke 11:10

I have the promise to receive my request.

Revelation 3:20

Jesus Christ is at the door of my heart, calling me. If I open my heart to Him, then He comes inside me and dine His Word with me.

1 Corinthians 6:17

When I joined myself to Jesus, I am one Spirit with Him and He with me.

2 Corinthians 3:17

Jesus is the Spirit and with Him is freedom.

John 14:20

I am one with Jesus and the Father.

John 14:21

Jesus's commandment is to love one another, and He will manifest His grace to me.

John 14:23

Because I love Him, Christ and the Father live inside me.

John 17:11; 17: 21

Jesus prayer to the Father is that I be one with them, and they in me.

John 17:21

By joining in one with Christ and the Father, I testify that the Father has send Jesus to the world.

Romans 12:1

To present ourselves as a living sacrifice means to live as Christ had lived. Doing the will of the Father in physical, as well as spiritual submission.

Romans 12:2

My understanding must be made new, to think little of what the world wants me to be and do. The only way to renew our mind is by reading and learning what the Word of God wants us to learn.

1 Thessalonians 5:23

I am a spirit, have a soul and live in a body. I must keep each of then clean of contamination.

2 Corinthians 7:1

Therefore, having these promises, beloved, let us cleanse ourselves from all filthiness of the flesh and spirit, perfecting holiness in the fear of God.

Ephesians 1:17

I declare to the Father my wish to receive the gift of His spirit of wisdom and revelation in the knowledge of Him and Christ.

Ephesians 1:18

Anticipating the enlightening of my spiritual eyes in discerning the super abundance of His glory and my inheritance with the saints.

Ephesians 1:19

To know the exuberant manifestation of His mighty power toward me, His believer.

Ephesians 1:20
The fulfillment that worked in Christ resurrecting Him, as prophesied in Psalm 110:1,
"The Lord said to my Lord, 'Sit at My right hand, till I make Your enemies Your footstool.'"

Ephesians 1:21
Above Satan's principality and every spiritual power and dominion, and give Him a name above any name.

Ephesians 1:22
Jesus Christ is declared head of the church having everything under His feet.

Ephesians 1:23
The church believers in Christ are members of His spiritual body on earth.

Ephesians 3:16
I want to receive strength by His spirit in my inner man.

Ephesians 6:10
My spiritual strength comes from the Lord Jesus by His spirit.

1 Timothy 2:8
I want to pray anywhere lifting holy hands without wrath, or anger.

1 Thessalonians 5:9
My job is not to incite wrath, but to bring salvation through Jesus Christ.

James 1:19
This is how I should speak and behave.

James 1:20
Wrath does not work the righteousness of God.

Philippians 4:6
I don't need to be stressful, just ask Him in prayer humbly, with faith.

1 Peter 5:7
I dismiss all worry on Jesus for I know He loves me.

Philippians 4:7
My thinking must be guided by peace, not strife.

Philippians 4:8

This should be the focus of where our thinking should be.

2 Corinthians 10:3

Arms are not suitable weapons against our spiritual enemy.

2 Corinthians 10:4

God gives us His spiritual weapon to demolish strongholds. These weapons have divine powers.

2 Corinthians 10:5

We must surrender to Christ our meditations.

1 Corinthians 15:31

Daily I die to sin but live in Christ.

Galatians 2:20

I consider myself crucified with Christ, yet alive in Him.

Galatians 5:24

I in Christ Jesus and He in me.
My old life has died at the cross.

Romans 6:6

When Christ was on the cross, my old man was also with Him. My body of sin died together with Him. If I died with Christ, I am free of sin and live with Him.

Romans 6:7

Since I, my old man, had died then I am free of sin.

Romans 6:8

Having died with Christ, by faith we live with Him.

Romans 6:11

I feel dead to sin, yet alive in Christ.

Romans 6:14

I live under grace and not under law. Sin has no more power over me.

Romans 8:1

I live free of condemnation in Christ by living according to the Spirit.

Romans 8:2

The law of life in Christ Jesus has set me free from the law of sin and death.

2 Corinthians 5:17

Being in Christ Jesus, I am a new creation. My life starts as a spiritual baby in Him.

Ephesians 2:10

I am His workmanship. A worthy and righteous new creation in Him.

John 7:38

I believe in Him. Out of my heart will flow His word; that is the river of living waters.

2 Corinthians 5:14

Christ died for all of us because we were spiritually dead.

2 Corinthians 5:15

We are spiritually alive in Christ should live for Him and not for ourselves.

Romans 14:7

My life is for Christ from now on.

Romans 14:8

The wonderful promise of belonging to Christ in life or dead.

2 Corinthians 4:16

I always thought of this verse as having found the fountain of youth.

1 Peter 2:9

Four titles are given us why witness the word of God everywhere.

1 Peter 1:23

We have been reborn by the word of God.

1 Thessalonians 5:16

Always be joyful and thankful to the Lord.

1 Thessalonians 5:1

Speak to God or pray, He wants us to.

1 Thessalonians 5:18

By giving thanks we acknowledge by faith to receive His blessings though Christ Jesus.

Luke 24:45

I believe the only way to understand the Scriptures is if Christ the Lord, opens our hearts and minds.

Psalm 19:11
Warnings and rewards are in God's Word.

Psalm 19:12
Don't hide my faults so I can correct my errors.

Psalm 19:13
Remove pride and arrogance, and I will be free from rebellion.

Psalm 19:14
I wish my words and thoughts are pleasing to You Lord Jesus.

Psalm 103:1
My soul, spirit and body blesses You, O my Lord.

Psalm 103:2
My soul remembers His blessings.

Psalm 103:3
He forgives my sins and heals my diseases.

Psalm 103:4
He rescued me from the death.

And surrenders me with His mercy and love.

Psalm 103:5
    He keeps me strong and healthy.

1 Corinthians 15:57
    If not for Jesus Christ, our Lord and Savior, we wouldn't have victory over the enemy of our souls.

Chapter 12

Two Destinations, One choice

Here is a teaching of Jesus for us:

> *Then the kingdom of heaven shall be likened to ten virgins who took their lamps and went out to meet their bridegroom. Now five of them were wise, and five were foolish. Those who were foolish took their lamps and took no oil with them, but the wise took oil in their vessels with their lamps. But while the bridegroom was delayed, they all slumbered and slept. And at midnight a cry was heard: 'Behold, the bridegroom is coming; go out to meet him!'' Then all those virgins arose and trimmed their lamps. And the foolish said to the wise, give us some of your oil, for our lamps are going out. But the wise answered, saying, "No, lest there should not be enough for us*

and you; but go rather to those who sell, and buy for yourselves." And while they went to buy, the bridegroom came, and those who were ready went in with him to the wedding; and the door was shut. Afterward the other virgins came also saying, "Lord, Lord, open to us!" But he answered and said, "Assuredly, I say to you, I do not know you." Watch therefore, for you know neither the day nor the hour in which the Son of Man is coming. (Mathew 25:1-13)

My interpretation: The ten virgins is the church. Those of us that believe in Jesus Christ as our Lord and Savior. The oil represents the Holy Spirit. The lamps is the abundance of the filling of the Holy Spirit in us.

The five foolish virgins are those Christians that don't have a constant fellowship with the Lord. They neglect their Christian life. They are lukewarm all their lives. They are neither cold nor hot.

The bridegroom is the Lord Jesus. The wedding is of the Lamb in His kingdom. Half the church is prepared to go with the Lord while the other half is not. To which half do you belong?

"And anyone not found written in the Book of Life was cast into the lake of fire" (Revelation 20:15).

The New Life in Christ

But I saw no temple in it, for the Lord God Almighty and the Lamb are its temple. The city had no need of the sun nor of the moon to shine in it for the glory of God illuminated it. The Lamb is its light. And the nations of those who are saved shall walk in its light, and the kings of the earth bring their glory and honor into it. Its gate shall not be shut at all by day (there shall be no night there). And they shall bring the glory and the honor of the nations into it. But there shall by no means enter it anything that defiles, or causes an abomination or a lie, but only those who are written in the Lamb's Book of Life. (Revelation 21:22–27)

How Do I Feel Today?

It is my desire that in your spirit, you have peace with Jesus and the Father as I have. I found that reading the Bible is the best way to know about God's fervent love toward us, His creation. God's desire is that we grow in Him. That is to increase our knowledge of Him and Christ, His Son, just as we have developed physically growing in our bodies from childhood to adults. God wants us to grow in our knowledge of Him.

For that reason, Jesus sent the Holy Spirit to be with us to teach us and remind us all the things He spoke to His disciples.

I want to end this book with a reminder of how important is to our lives to choose WHO WILL I SERVE.

The End

About the Author

Enrique Tomás Martinovic was born in Rosario, Argentina, on August 19, 1942. His studies where completed in different schools and colleges both state and private.

His major since his early years has been always in the field of commerce. His father had a career in business before his birth and later a store. So that seemed to him like the right profession to follow for his life.

At the age of twenty-one, he met Marta. After a brief two and half months of courtship, they married. That was September 19, 1963. It was at that time when his first experiences in Christian life began.

In 1970, they migrated to the United States. In 1986, they both became US citizens. Throughout those years, they had two children in Argentina and six in the United States. The struggle was tremendous, but the love of God and His care for Enrique remains infinite.

During all those years, Enrique had several experiences in his relationship with the Lord, Jesus Christ. Throughout his life, the heavenly Father has guided his journey. He has protected him and strengthened his faith and conviction. Finally, it became a burning fire inside him. He longed to share his experiences of the love of God with others. His wish is that his readers have a similar relationship with the Creator like the one he has.

CPSIA information can be obtained
at www.ICGtesting.com
Printed in the USA
FSHW012009020721
82937FS